Copyright: Really Useful Map Company (HK) Ltd.
Published By: Robert Frederick Ltd.
4 North Parade Bath, England.
First Published: 2005

Designed and packaged by
Q2A Creative
Printed in India.

DISCOVER
BUGS

Contents

Bug World

Bugs are creepy, crawly creatures that live in the garden, under stones, and even in your house. Commonly called insects, bugs are small, six-legged animals. There are over a million species or types of insects – much more than all the animals and plant types put together!

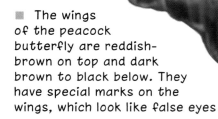

■ The wings of the peacock butterfly are reddish-brown on top and dark brown to black below. They have special marks on the wings, which look like false eyes

■ A dragonfly has four large wings that look like fine gauze. As it flies through the air, it holds its legs together to form a basket in which other insects are caught. The dragonfly can eat while flying

Living zones

Look around anywhere, and you are sure to find a bug. Insects can live almost anywhere on earth – from hot tropical jungles to snow-capped mountains and scorching deserts. They can be found in caves and burrows deep in the earth, or flying high in the sky. Some insects can even live on an animal's body, or inside it.

Tasty bite

Most insects feed on plants. But bugs usually create no fuss about food and can eat almost anything. They are known to feed on fabrics, plaster, cork, face powder, other living things, and even toothpaste!

Secret of success!

Bugs appeared on earth long before humans. The secret of their ability to survive in just about any condition lies in their small size, tough outer skeleton and adaptability. Bugs are not choosy about the places they live in or the things they eat. Bugs also have short lives. They quickly become adults and give birth to a large number of babies – each of them better survivors than their parents.

FACT FILE

Smallest
Dwarf beetle; 0.25 mm
Largest
Atlas moth; it has a wingspan of about 25 cm (9.8 inches)
Heaviest
Goliath beetle; weighs up to 96.4 g (3.4 ounces)
Longest
Stick insect; females grow over 36 cm (14.2 inches) in length

■ The black or black-and-orange burying beetles look out for dead mice and other small animals. They bury these animals so they can feed on them

INTERESTING FACT!

Most insects are less than 6 mm (0.24 inches) long. The smallest ones include hairy-winged dwarf beetles. They can easily crawl through the eye of a needle, and are barely visible to the human eye!

Bugging us

We are constantly at war with insects. They annoy us, bite us, infect us with diseases, eat our food, and damage our property. But not all insects are harmful. A lot of them are of great value to us. Some help in pollination, while others serve as food for fish, birds and many other animals. In fact, life on earth may not exist if all the insects were to disappear.

■ Despite their names, velvet ants are actually a species of wasp. The female velvet ant does not have any wings

Inside Story

Although they come in various shapes, sizes and colours, all bugs have a common body structure. Their body is divided into three main parts – head, thorax and abdomen. All bugs have six legs, arranged in three pairs. They also have a pair of antennae and a tough, shell-like outer covering. Some bugs even have wings.

Armour suit

Bugs have a shell-like outer covering over their soft bodies. This outer covering is called the exoskeleton. It is usually light and strong, and serves as a suit of armour that protects the bug. The muscles of the bug are attached to the inside wall of the exoskeleton.

■ A human bone grows with age. But like in all other bugs, the exoskeleton of a cockroach also does not grow as it gets older. Hence, the exoskeleton becomes too tight and needs to be shed. The bug forms a new suit of armour underneath before it crawls out of the old suit

INTERESTING FACT!

When insects walk, they usually move the middle leg on one side, with the front and hind legs on the opposite side. In this way, they are always firmly supported – like a three-legged stool.

A Madagascar hissing cockroach

Abdomen

A bug's abdomen contains its organs, which are very different from a human being's. Air enters the insect through a few pores in the exoskeleton. These pores are called spiracles. Oxygen is distributed to all areas of the body through breathing tubes. In humans, blood flows through special tubes called blood vessels. In bugs, though, blood flows throughout the body cavity.

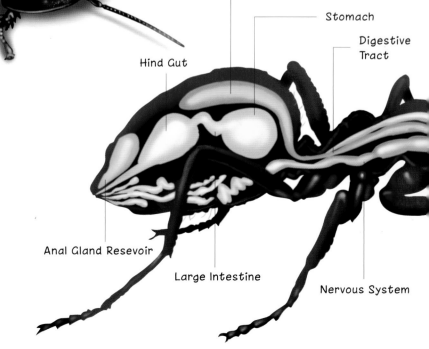

Social Stomach

Stomach

Digestive Tract

Hind Gut

Anal Gland Resevoir

Large Intestine

Nervous System

FACT FILE

Fastest-flying insect
Dragonfly; 95 km/h
Longest flight
Butterflies and locusts can
fly continuously for well over
160 km. Tiny fruit flies can
fly more than five hours
Shortest flight
Honeybees can fly only for
15 minutes at a time
Wing speed
Large-winged butterflies
beat their wings 4 to 20
times per second; houseflies,
about 200 times; and some
midges about 1,000 times
per second
Fastest-moving insect
Cockroach; 5.40 km/h

■ insects that chew have powerful grinding jaws called mandibles. The jaws work sideways, not up and down as in humans. The jaws are also modified for sucking

Heady matter

A bug's head includes mouthparts, eyes and the antennae. The mouth has special structures for feeding, which allow the bug to chew or suck. Most adult insects have two enormous eyes, with a pair of antennae between them. They use these antennae to smell, taste and even hear.

Brain

Eye

Mandible Gland Reservoir

■ Bugs have compound eyes. While humans have just one lens, insects can have thousands of separate lenses. These combine to form a complete picture of what an insect sees

Midzone

The thorax is the middle section of a bug's body. It supports the three pairs of legs and the wings, if present. Bugs can use their legs for running, grasping, digging or swimming.

Changing Times

Nearly every insect starts life as an egg. After hatching, the insect begins to grow and develops into an adult. During this process, most insects go through a series of amazing changes in form. The entire cycle – from egg to adult – takes only a few days for some species, and as long as 17 years for others.

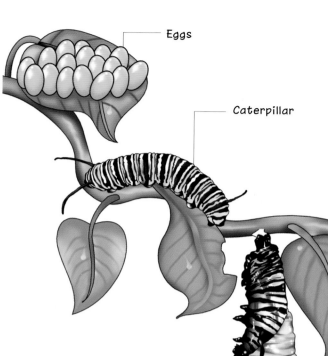

Eggs

Caterpillar

Caterpillar entering pupal stage

Growing up

After an egg hatches, it follows one of three patterns of growth and development, depending on its type. The simplest cycle occurs in a few kinds like silverfish and springtails. When the eggs of these insects hatch, the young ones look exactly like their parents, only smaller. These are called nymphs.

■ This is a trilobite larva, which is actually a female bug that grows to maturity while retaining their juvenile or larval form

Changing form

Other insects have a far different pattern of growth and development. The young look different from their parents and are called larvae. They change in form as they develop into adults. This change is called metamorphosis.

■ Cicadas plant their eggs in tree branches. On hatching, the nymphs fall to the ground and scurry into the soil, settling near the tree roots. They feed on the sap for 7 years, moulting as they grow older. This means they shed the old exoskeleton and get a new one

Types of metamorphosis

There are two kinds of metamorphosis. In incomplete metamorphosis, the nymphal stages look like the adult except that they don't have wings. The nymphs may also have a different colour than the adults. In complete metamorphosis, on the other hand, young bugs do not at all look like the adults. The nymphs often live in different habitats, and feed on different things.

Adult Butterfly

Adult butterfly
coming out
of pupa

Pupa about
to open

■ After a larva completes its growth,
it stops eating and spins a cocoon – a
protective covering – around its body. It
then becomes a pupa. Inside the covering, it is
broken down and re-formed into adult organs.
After the change is complete, the pupal
covering cracks open and the adult flies out

Eggs of all shapes

Insect eggs have a variety of shapes and colour patterns, but most are oval or round and are pale- or cream-coloured. Insects lay their eggs singly or in batches. They usually lay them on or near food, which the young eat after they hatch.

INTERESTING FACT!

A pair of houseflies could produce millions of babies, if all of them lived! Attacks by parasites, predators, lack of food supply, and other factors prevent many of them from surviving.

■ The cockroach's
egg case is the size
and shape of a baked
bean. It can contain
from 10 to 20 eggs

Know your Bugs

All small animals that crawl are not bugs. A spider is not an insect, and neither is a centipede. In fact, only those crawling creatures that have six legs and a body divided into three parts are called insects.

Caught in a web

Spiders differ from bugs in many ways. While spiders have eight legs, bugs have six. A spider's body is divided into only two main parts, whereas a bug has three parts. Most bugs have wings and antennae, but spiders do not.

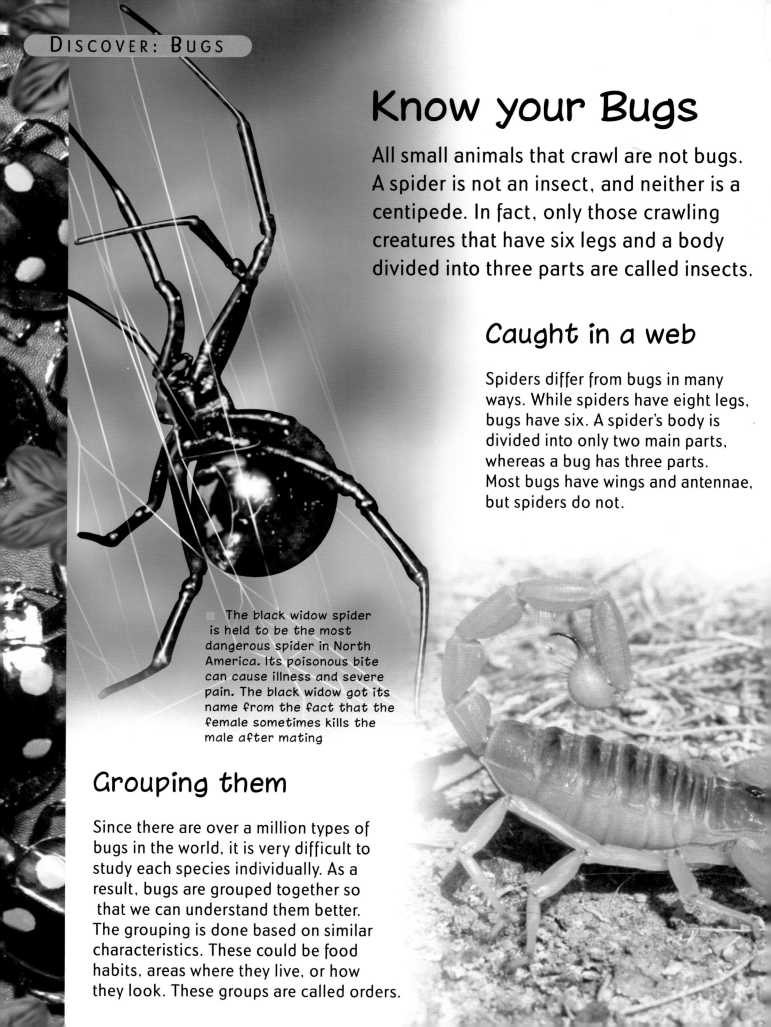

The black widow spider is held to be the most dangerous spider in North America. Its poisonous bite can cause illness and severe pain. The black widow got its name from the fact that the female sometimes kills the male after mating

Grouping them

Since there are over a million types of bugs in the world, it is very difficult to study each species individually. As a result, bugs are grouped together so that we can understand them better. The grouping is done based on similar characteristics. These could be food habits, areas where they live, or how they look. These groups are called orders.

FACT FILE

Life span
Tarantula
Can live up to 30 years
Queen termite
Known to live up to 50 years
Locust
Up to 17 years
Wood beetle
40 years
Mayfly
Just a few hours or one day

■ Although both centipedes and millipedes look similar, they are very different. Centipedes, like this giant desert centipede, can grow up to 20 cm in length, while millipedes are not longer than 10 cm. Most centipedes are venomous, while millipedes roll into a ball when threatened

INTERESTING FACT!

Centipedes and millipedes are not bugs. They have narrow bodies divided into segments. Each section has one or two pairs of legs. Centipedes can have 15 to 175 pairs of legs, while millipedes can have up to 380.

Some confusion

Entomologists, or people who study bugs, do not agree on the number of orders that exist. Some may consider a certain group of bugs as a single order, but others might regard it as two or more orders. For this reason, some say that there are more than 30 orders, and others list fewer than 25.

■ Scorpions have a poisonous sting at the end of their tails, capable of killing humans as well. Scorpions are not bugs, though

Naming game

The orders are arranged according to how bugs have developed over millions of years. Since most orders are based on similar features, the name of the order tells us about a particular feature. The feature is usually given at the end of the name as a suffix. Thus, the suffix -ura means tail; -ptera, wings; and aptera, wingless.

Bug Senses

Bugs are much more sensitive than humans. These creatures depend on their senses of touch, hearing, smell, sight and taste to find their way home, locate food, and protect themselves. While bugs have special sense organs, the most crucial is the antenna. They suffer a lot if you remove or damage the antenna, and some can even become helpless.

■ Some kinds of bugs – including ants, bees and wasps – have taste organs on their antennae. They touch the food with their antennae, and eat it only if they like the taste. Other bugs – including butterflies, some moths and flies and honeybees – taste with their feet!

Many lenses

Most bugs have two large compound eyes on their head. While humans have just one lens in their eyes that enables them to focus on objects, bugs have many lenses. Each eye is made up of tiny, six-sided lenses that fit together like a honeycomb.

Smelly factor

A bug's antenna also helps it to smell things. It uses its sense of smell to look for food, find its way about, and locate places to lay eggs. Ants and bees recognise other members of their colony by their odour.

■ Bugs like the dragonfly can see only a short distance. Objects more than one metre away appear as a blur to them. But they can see quick movements as well as recognise colours. Bugs have no eyelids and their eyes are always open

Touchy creatures

Bugs can feel things better than us. They sense the air around them with the hairs and spines that cover their body and antennae. Bugs can even feel a change in the air around them. That is why no matter how carefully you move your hand towards a fly, it will always fly away!

■ Bristles, or fine hairs, on the antennae and the legs help the bug to hear, smell, taste and even feel objects!

■ A bug's ears can be located almost anywhere on the body, but never in the head. For instance, the narrow-beaked katydid has ears on its legs!

INTERESTING FACT!

Bugs do not have real voices. Many of them rub body parts against each other to make sounds. Crickets rub their legs together to make chirping sounds, while bees make a humming noise by flapping their wings rapidly.

Hear a whisper

Most bugs can hear sounds that are either too soft or too loud for humans. But only a few types of bugs have true ears. Others hear with the delicate hairs on their antennae, as also with their bodies.

Attack and Defence

A bug's life is filled with dangers. It may be eaten by other bugs, birds or animals. Cold weather may kill it; else, a dry spell may kill the plants it eats. People are also a threat to it. Hence, to fight for survival, bugs have developed special means of defence.

Scooting away

Bugs have many protection skills. The easiest way is to escape, and quickly fly, leap or scamper away. Some caterpillars and beetles play dead, or adopt threatening postures to frighten the enemy. They also adopt special poses to attack and kill other bugs.

■ The mantis, also called the "praying mantis", holds its front legs as if it were praying. It uses its arm-like forelegs to grasp and capture its prey. In fact, since the colour of its body blends in with the plant it is on, the mantis is missed by both its prey and predator

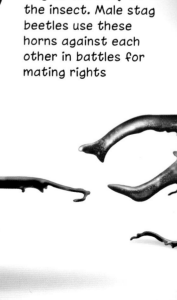

■ Male stag beetles have oddly enlarged jaws. They look like the horns of a male deer and can be as long as the body of the insect. Male stag beetles use these horns against each other in battles for mating rights

Weapons of war

Most bugs have powerful weapons with which to keep enemies away. Thus, bees, wasps and some ants have poisonous stings. Certain ants, horseflies and other bugs can pinch with their powerful jaws. Caterpillars often have hollow body hairs filled with poison. These hairs break at the slightest touch, releasing the poison. Stinkbugs, lacewings and carrion beetles give off foul odours. Some butterflies, moths and other bugs are also protected simply because they taste bad to their predators!

Many spiders eat each other. Most female spiders are larger and stronger than male spiders, and occasionally eat the males

Mimics for life

Some bugs are great mimics – that is, they resemble other bugs. This often protects weak bugs, which look like stronger bugs. To illustrate, because a viceroy butterfly resembles the monarch butterfly, birds leave it alone, because the monarch tastes unpleasant to them.

Colouring camouflage

Some bugs also escape their enemies because either their colour or form blends with the surroundings. This is called camouflaging. When resting on tree trunks, many moths look like bark or bird droppings. Stick bugs and some caterpillars resemble twigs.

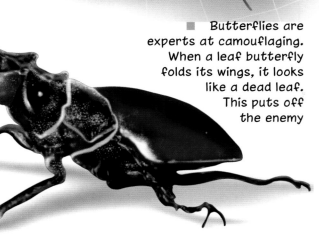

■ Butterflies are experts at camouflaging. When a leaf butterfly folds its wings, it looks like a dead leaf. This puts off the enemy

Bees and Wasps

While most animals on earth live on their own, a special group of bugs stays in huge colonies. They are called social bugs. Termites, ants, bees and wasps are all social bugs. Some of their colonies are far better-organised than even human settlements.

All in a family

Social bugs live in communities wherein each member depends upon the other. Those living together are often part of the same family. For example, the 60,000 to 80,000 bees in a hive are all born from one queen. So are the millions of termites that may make up a termite colony.

■ A hornet is a kind of wasp that lives in large paper nests that are shaped like an upside-down pear. These usually hang from branches or leaves

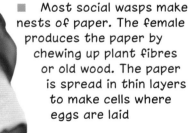

■ Most social wasps make nests of paper. The female produces the paper by chewing up plant fibres or old wood. The paper is spread in thin layers to make cells where eggs are laid

Shared work

Each member of a colony does the work given to it. The queen's job is to lay eggs. The adults in the colony, called workers, feed and care for the young. Termites have both male and female workers, though all the workers among ants, bees and wasps, are females.

Male zone

Males are found in a colony of social bugs only for limited periods of time. The males' only job is to mate with the queen, after which they die. In bees, the males are called drones, while in termite colonies they are the kings!

◼ Bees eat only nectar. Wasps can feed on other bugs and human food as well

INTERESTING FACT!

Social bugs communicate with one another with the use of sound, touch and scent. Honeybees use a form of dance to tell other members of the hive the direction and distance of where food is to be found.

Different tasks

Each colony member performs a specialised task. Nurses look after the young and soldiers defend the colony from attacks by enemies. Some workers search for food, while others enlarge and clean the nest.

◼ Cuckoo bees invade the nests of bumblebees and lay eggs there. The bumblebees raise the cuckoos' young as their own

Ants and Termites

Ants are among the most successful social bugs. While they may look small and simple, they can have the most complex way of life. The division of work in colonies as well as the means to get food can vastly differ for them.

Special mounds

Termites construct extremely large and elaborate mounds to house their colonies. These mounds can have various forms and are as hard as concrete. On the inside, mounds may have chimneys, a nursery, waste-disposal chambers and a special cell for the queen.

■ The inside of a termite mound is divided into many chambers and galleries. In the centre is a closed cell, where the queen dwells

■ The soldier termites are wingless and blind. They are larger in built than the workers, with a huge head, powerful jaws and strong legs

Up in arms

Army ants march across huge distances on land and eat other bugs. A single parade of army ants looks so formidable that even bigger creatures are intimidated. Due to their sheer number, army ants can also attack mice and lizards. If a prey is not able to escape the circle of ants, it is quickly torn to bits.

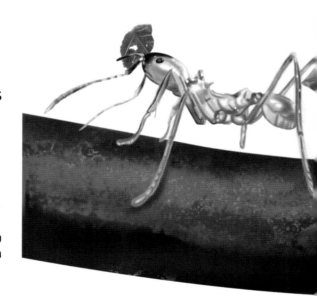

■ Leafcutter ants continually collect leaves, which they cut into tiny pieces for the mushroom to grow on

FACT FILE

Termite mounds can be
as high as 6 m (20 feet)
Largest ant
over 2.5 cm (1 inch) long
Smallest ant
about 0.1 cm (0.04 inch)
long
Queen ant
lives 10-20 years; workers,
1-5 years; while male ants
survive for just a few months

Slave drivers

Certain kinds of ants keep aphids, caterpillars or other bugs, which they "milk" for food. Many ants raid other ants' nests and carry off the young, which they bring up as slaves.

■ Weaver ants build nests in trees by attaching leaves together. Bridges of workers first pull in the leaves. These leaves are then sewed up by pressing silk-producing larvae against them

INTERESTING FACT!

Ants "talk" to one another by giving off chemicals called pheromones. An ant may lay a scent trail from a newly discovered food supply to its nest. The other workers then follow the trail to the food.

Self-made or thieves

Ants have different ways of gathering food. Harvester ants collect seeds, which are stored in their nests. Thief ants live by stealing food from other ants. Some other species, such as leafcutter ants, actually grow their own food. They cultivate tiny mushroom gardens in their nests.

Winged Wonders

The butterfly is among the most beautiful of all bugs. They have delicate and very colourful wings. Butterflies and moths belong to the same order of winged bugs. They are the only bugs to have scales on their wings.

■ Most butterflies rest with their wings held upright over their bodies. Moths, however, rest with their wings spread out flat

Moth vs butterfly

Although grouped together, moths are not as beautiful as butterflies. Moths have plump, furry bodies, while butterflies are slender. Moths also do not have knobs on their antennae like butterflies do. Moreover, while butterflies fly during the day, moths prefer nights.

Before take-off

Butterflies and moths cannot fly if their body temperature is less than 30 °C. If the temperature is low, they need to warm up. The bugs either bask in the sun or shake their wings to build up heat.

■ The Heliconid butterfly is also known as the "passion flower" butterfly. It feeds on the poisonous leaves of the passion-flower. This makes it inedible for other animals

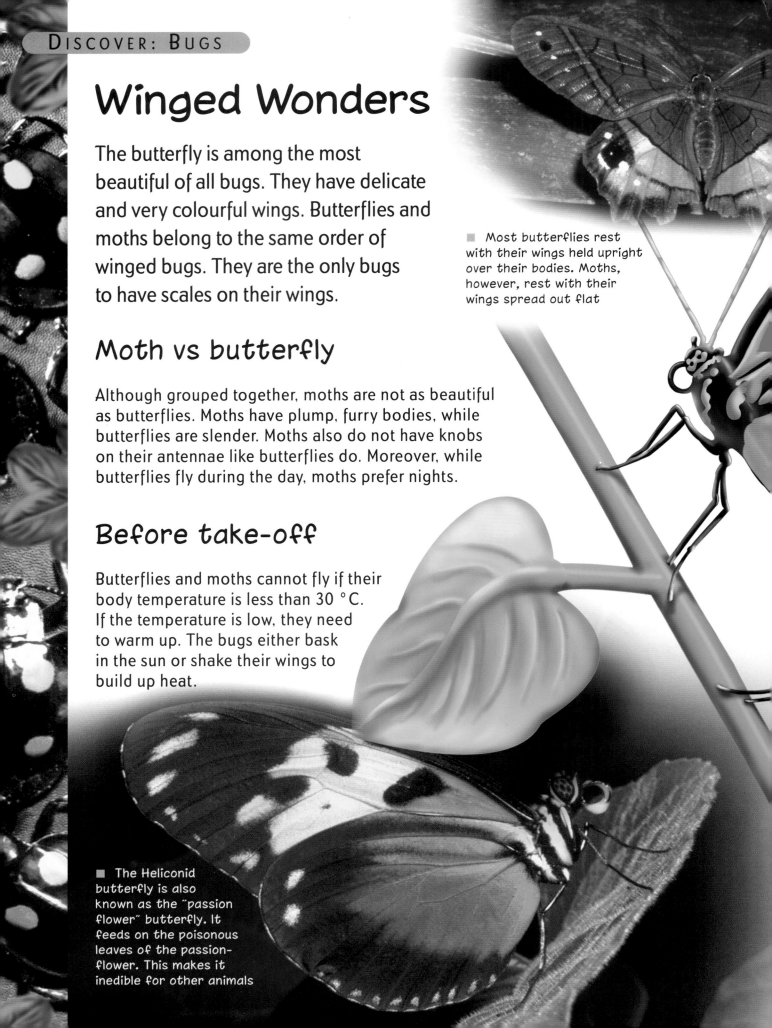

Hungry caterpillar

Butterflies and moths undergo a complete change while going through four different life stages. They start life as an egg. The larva or caterpillar hatches from the egg and feeds on leaves or flowers. As it grows, the caterpillar loses its outer skin – in other words, it molts many times.

FACT FILE
Types
15,000 to 20,000
Largest
Queen Alexandra's birdwing of Papua New Guinea; wingspread of about 28 cm (11 inches)
Smallest
Western pygmy blue of North America; wingspread of about 1 cm (0.39 inch)
Fastest
Some skippers can fly over 48 kph (30mph)
Slowest
Flies at about 8 kph (5mph)

■ Butterflies attract each other with the colour patterns on their wings. The female begins laying eggs within a few hours, but the male dies

Resting stage

After reaching its full size, the caterpillar turns into a pupa. The pupa is motionless, which is why this is often called the "resting" stage. The adult butterfly is slowly formed within the shell. This stage can last from a few days to over a year.

■ Satyrid butterflies, also called wood nymphs, fly at low heights and in a zigzag manner. On sensing danger, the butterflies stay motionless with closed wings. If the danger continues, they fly away

INTERESTING FACT!

In addition to colour and shape, the fragrance of flowers is what really draws butterflies to a garden. Flowers with the strongest perfume are most appealing to a butterfly's sensitive sense of smell.

Along Came a Spider

One of the most common crawling creatures on earth is the spider. But unlike what most people think, spiders are not bugs. Rather, they belong to a completely different group of animals called arachnids. Scorpions also belong to this group.

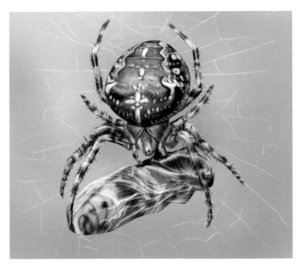

Living zones

Just like bugs, spiders too can live anywhere. Spiders are found in fields, woods, swamps, caves and deserts. Spiders help people by eating harmful bugs. They eat grasshoppers and locusts, which destroy crops, and flies and mosquitoes, which carry diseases.

■ A spider never gets caught in its own web. The spider walks across the web, holding on to the silk lines with a special hooked claw on each foot

■ Most spiders enclose their eggs in a sac. The egg sac is a bag made of a special kind of silk. Some spiders hang their sac in a web. Others attach it to leaves or plants. Still others carry it with them. Spiderlings hatch inside the egg sac

Spot the difference

The difference between bugs and spiders can be seen from their body structure. All bugs have six legs, but spiders have eight. While the body of an insect is divided into three parts, a spider's body has only two segments. In addition, most bugs have wings and antennae (feelers), but spiders do not.

FACT FILE

Types
more than 30,000
Largest
South American tarantula,
25 centimetres long
Smallest
an orbweb from Samoa
0.43 mm long, about the
size of a pinhead
Average eggs layed
100, can go up to 2,000

Spinning magic

Spiders produce silk for their web through special glands. The web is spun through short, finger-like organs called spinnerets, which are attached to the abdomen. A spider can have two, four, or six spinnerets. The tip of a spinneret is covered with tubes, through which liquid silk flows from the glands. The silk later hardens into a thread.

Web of death

Spiders love to feed on bugs and spin webs to catch them. Even bugs that are larger and stronger than spiders cannot escape from the threads of a spider's web.

■ Hunting spiders have good eyesight at short distances. Web-building spiders, on the other hand, have poor eyesight. Their eyes are used for detecting changes in light

INTERESTING FACT!

More than 150 spiders were used in the movie "Spider-Man." They were specially picked for the role. Those who made it to the big screen had the best spider behaviour!

■ Orb weavers spin the most beautiful webs. Many orb weavers spin a new web every night. And it takes them just about an hour to do so. These weavers often wrap their victims in sheets, just like mummies

Knights in Shining Armour

Beetles are the toughest looking bugs around. Unlike other bugs, adult beetles have a pair of special front wings called elytra. They form a leathery cover, protecting the beetle's body. Beetles are called the armoured tanks of the insect world, because of these hard wings and the shell-like skeleton.

Amazing variety

Beetles live everywhere on earth except in the oceans. They vary greatly in shape, colour and size. Some, such as click beetles and fireflies, are long and slender. Others, including ladybirds, are round. Most beetles are brown, black or dark red in colour though some can have bright, shiny rainbow colours.

■ Fungus beetles feed on spores of fungi. They also mess up the areas they live with their waste and cast skins

■ Weevils also called snout beetles. The mouths of adult weevils are at the tip of a long snout, which is used to bore into fruits, seeds and other plant parts. The larvae have no legs and feed on the inside of fruits and nuts and are called borers. Many weevils are known to destroy crops

Legs for work

Like their shape and colour, the legs of a beetle also vary. Each of the six legs usually has claws at the end. Beetles that are fast runners have long, slender legs. Others have short and stout legs, with flat pads that helps them walk on slippery surfaces. Digging beetles have tooth-like projections on their legs to scrape away soil. Most swimming beetles have flat, hind legs.

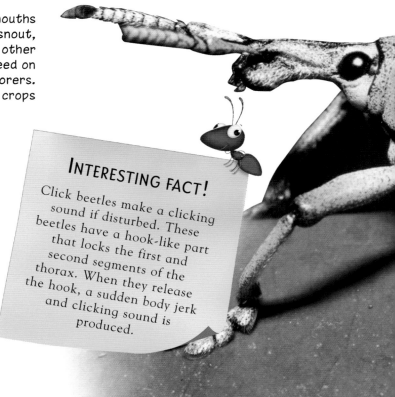

INTERESTING FACT!

Click beetles make a clicking sound if disturbed. These beetles have a hook-like part that locks the first and second segments of the thorax. When they release the hook, a sudden body jerk and clicking sound is produced.

FACT FILE

Smallest: Feather-winged beetles, less than 0.5 millimetres long.
Largest: the Goliath beetle of Africa grows to about 13 centimetres
Strongest: American burying beetles can lift 200 times their own weight
Hottest: Bombardier beetles can shoot a hot, smelly liquid, 100ì C in temperature, from their abdomen

■ Scarab beetles such as dung beetles and tumblebugs feed on dung. They roll the dung into balls and bury it in soil. Females lay one egg in the ball of dung. Some Scarab like June beetles and Japanese beetles eat crops

Mixed bag

Many beetles feed on crops, trees or stored food causing a lot of damage. Such bugs are called pests. However, some beetles are helpful to people. For example, ladybirds and certain other beetles save crops by eating bugs such as aphids. Other beetles, like the dung beetle, are important because they eat dead plants and animals, clearing the environment.

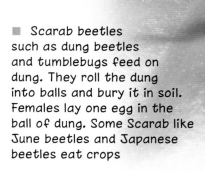

■ Darkling beetles feed on plants and like to walk around. But when disturbed, they assume a head-down and tail-up position. If handled roughly, they emit a dark-coloured, foul-smelling fluid. This behaviour is enough to ward off most predators

Enemy protection

Beetles have many enemies, including birds, reptiles and other bugs. Most beetles protect themselves by biting, hiding or flying away. Some beetles produce a bad smell that puts off predators.

Ballet Dancers

Not all bugs are short, round and ugly. Butterflies, dragonflies and mayflies are very pretty. They have four lacy wings and a slim and long tail that trails behind them. The wings shimmer and gleam in the sunlight when the insect flies. These bugs looks so graceful while flying that you can even call them the "ballet dancers" of the bug world!

Nymph's tale

Young mayflies are called nymphs or naiads. Mayflies lay their eggs in streams and ponds. The nymphs breathe through gills, feed on water plants and live for a few months to two years. They shed their skin when they leave the water, and become winged subimagos, or subadults. Mayflies are the only bugs to go through this stage. After many hours, the subimago becomes a full-grown adult.

■ Mayflies are commonly called dayflies because of their short lives. Adult mayflies live for only a few hours or a few days

■ The dragonfly can hover in mid-air by flapping its wings. It eats other bugs, catching them while flying

Keen eyes

The dragonfly's long, slender body may be red, green, or blue, with white, yellow, or black markings. Large eyes, which look like beads, cover most of its head. The eyes are very sharp and can see objects over two metres away.

FACT FILE

Biggest living dragonfly
Megaloprepus coerulatus;
wingspan about 19 cm
(7 inches)
Bulkiest
Petalura ingentissima
Smallest
Nannophya pygmaea;
15 mm (1.5 cm) long,
wingspan about 20 mm
(2 cm)
Average speed
16 kmph (10 mph)

Masking lip

Dragonfly nymphs remain
in the water for one to
five years. They have
a thick body and a big
head and mouth, but
no wings. They have a
folding lower lip, called
a mask, which is half as
long as their bodies. The
lip has jaw-like hooks at
the end and can move
out to capture prey.

■ Dobson flies resemble
dragonflies. However, they
cannot fly as well as
dragonflies. Moreover, unlike
dragonflies, dobson flies can
fold their wings over their
backs when not in flight

INTERESTING FACT!

Fireflies have a unique form
of communication – light!
The light organs in a firefly
are located on the underside
of the abdomen, the last
section of an insect's body.
A chemical reaction in the
light organs produces the
firefly's light.

Flying with the wind

The front and back wings of the dragonfly
move separately, allowing them to stop and
change direction in mid-air. This also helps
them to fly at higher speeds. While resting,
the dragonflies holds its wings open. Their
back wings are broader than the front ones.

True Bugs

True bugs occur all over the world. Unlike most other bugs, true bugs have both piercing and sucking mouthparts. These are found in a long, beak-like structure on the body. True bugs mostly feed on plant juices, though some can also suck blood from animals or other bugs.

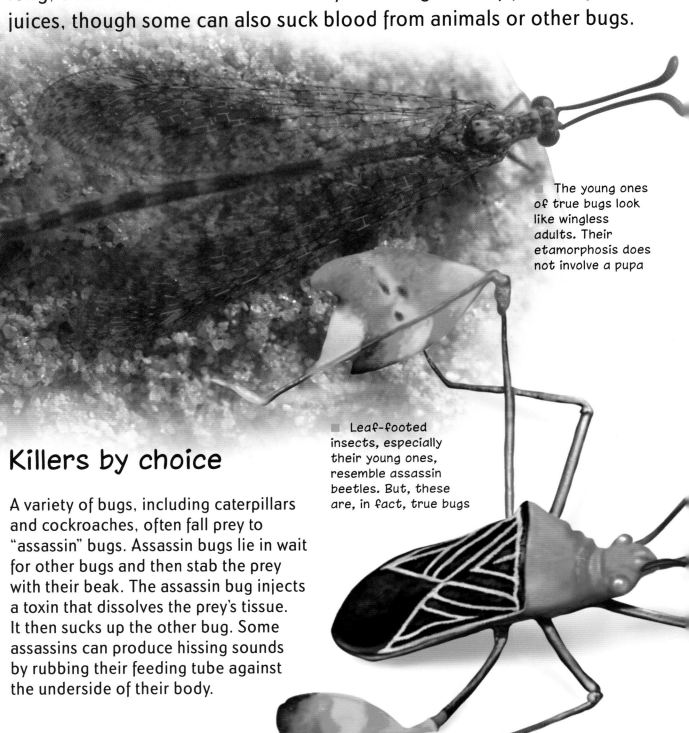

The young ones of true bugs look like wingless adults. Their etamorphosis does not involve a pupa

Leaf-footed insects, especially their young ones, resemble assassin beetles. But, these are, in fact, true bugs

Killers by choice

A variety of bugs, including caterpillars and cockroaches, often fall prey to "assassin" bugs. Assassin bugs lie in wait for other bugs and then stab the prey with their beak. The assassin bug injects a toxin that dissolves the prey's tissue. It then sucks up the other bug. Some assassins can produce hissing sounds by rubbing their feeding tube against the underside of their body.

FACT FILE
Number of species
Over 80,000
Length
1 mm (0.04 inch) to 11 cm
(4.3 inches)

Half wings

True bugs have a kind of "half" wing – with the front wing divided into a leathery hard part and a membranous softer part. These wing covers are held over the back and are often partly folded.

Walking on water

Many true bugs are aquatic. These water striders move on water with their feet barely touching the surface. They detect the ripples of other bugs on the water and run quickly to capture and kill the prey.

■ Most cockroaches, like this rainforest cockroach, have wings. However, female cockroaches, nymphs and some species like the Madagascar hissing cockroach do not have wings. Although some winged cockroaches can fly, others are unable to do so

Pest problems

Many stink bugs and shield bugs are agricultural pests. They suck plant juices and damage crop production. These bugs are present in large populations. They are also resistant to the sprays that are used to kill such bugs.

■ Some bugs are capable of producing a foul-smelling chemical with the glands on the sides of their bodies. They are known as stink bugs

INTERESTING FACT!

Some true bugs are eaten by humans. A variety of water bug is used in Chinese food. In Thailand, the giant water bug is a delicacy. It is either eaten whole or prepared as sauce for dipping.

Camouflage Specialists

Some bugs, like the leaf and stick bugs, are masters of camouflage – that is, they can blend into their surroundings. It is very difficult to spot these bugs in the forest. This special feature helps bugs to hide from enemies. It also allows them to sneak up quietly on their prey.

Blowing in the wind

In order to completely blend into its surroundings, the leaf insect walks by gently swaying its whole body from side to side. It then looks like a leaf blowing in the wind. This perfect camouflage allows the leaf insect to be active during the day.

■ Colour plays a major role in camouflage. But it is also important for the insect to remain motionless. The katydid has mastered this art perfectly. A katydid sitting on a leaf can be seen only upon careful examination

FACT FILE

Leaf insect
Average length 14 cm (6 inches); can be as long as 25 cm (10 inches)
Stick insect
Average length 10-15 cm (4-6 inches); can be as long as 52 cm (20 inches)

Hiding in branches

As their names suggest, stick bugs look like branches. You can spot them by looking for a branch that is out of line or attached to the outside edges of leaves. Stick bugs are usually drab in colour, but one type of stick bug has a stunning sky-blue colour.

Under leaves

Leaf bugs hang from the underside of tree leaves. At first they look like dried, dead leaves and are tough to spot. Their colour can range from pale green to dark brown, depending on the colour of the leaves.

Protection sprays

Some camouflage bugs also have other defence mechanisms to shoo away the enemy. The peppermint stick bug sprays an irritating fluid at its predators, the smell of which is much like a peppermint. The sprays can also be foul-smelling.

■ Certain types of stick bugs have projections along the body, which look like the thorns of a plant

■ Walking stick bugs are small and slow-moving. They feed on plant products

INTERESTING FACT!

Some leaf bugs have broad-ribbed wings that fold over the back in the shape of a leaf. These bugs can also have enlarged, leaf-like growths on the joint of their legs, giving them their particular name.

Garden Party

Every bug lover's favourite place is the garden. Among the bugs that can be found in a garden are grasshoppers, crickets and cicadas. These garden bugs are either green or brown in colour. They feed on plant products and the remains of other bugs.

Hopping and walking

Grasshoppers can hop, walk and fly. The long legs at the back are used for hopping and the bug can leap about 20 times the length of its body. The shorter front legs are used to hold the prey as well as to walk.

■ The cicada is a large-bodied, dark-coloured flying insect. When at rest, it holds the wings over the body like a tent. Male cicadas are the noisiest insects in the world

■ Most grasshoppers are green, olive green or brown in colour. But rainbow grasshoppers are very colourful

Eyeing around

A grasshopper has five eyes. Each side of the head has a large compound eye with thousands of single lenses. These eyes allow the bug to see all around. A grasshopper also has three small single eyes. One is above the base of the antenna, one below and one midway between the two antennae. No one knows what function these small eyes have.

FACT FILE

Grasshoppers lay
2 to 120 eggs at a time
They can be as long as
11 cm (4.5 inches)
They can jump to 20 times
its body length
Crickets
can be 2.5-7 cm
(0.9-3 inches) long

INTERESTING FACT!

Certain species of cicadas, called periodical cicadas, take 13-17 years to develop. Depending upon the species, the nymphs spend about 13-17 years underground before coming out to mate. The adult cicadas die soon after mating!

■ The Jerusalem cricket can be found in moist areas in deserts. It has a child-like face, because of which it is called "child of the earth" in some places

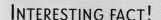

■ Grasshoppers are eaten in many countries. They are a good source of protein. Many countries also instruct army men to eat grasshoppers when they get lost and run out of food

Song of love

Male crickets are said to "sing" songs. And each kind of cricket has a different song. Some trill, while others make a series of chirps. Crickets produce a musical chirping sound by rubbing their two front wings together. It is this sound that leads female crickets to the male!

Cricket info

Crickets are related to grasshoppers but have many differences. The wings of most crickets lie flat over each other on top of their backs. Other crickets only have tiny wings, or are wingless. The slender antennae are much longer than the body in most of these bugs.

Venom and Stings

An insect bite, or a sting, can be very painful and poisonous. A bug uses its bite or sting for two purposes. The first is for protection from enemies. A bite can put off any enemy or even paralyse it. The other use of the sting is to get food. Bugs that feed on other bugs use this tactic.

Bee sting

Most bees depend on their stingers, or stings for defending their homes. The sting of a worker bee is straight, with hooks on it. When the bee thrusts the sting into the flesh, the hook holds tight and the stinger pulls out of the bee's body. Glands attached to the sting produce a poison, which is pumped in.

■ Scorpions perform dance-like movements while mating

Death of the worker

Queen bees have a smooth, curved sting that is used to kill other queens. Queens do not lose their stings like worker bees. A worker bee dies soon after losing its sting. Drones have no stings.

■ The earwig gets its name from the belief that it crawls into the ears of humans and lays eggs in their brains! However, this is not true. Earwigs are harmless to humans. But if carelessly handled, the insect can give you a painful pinch with its pincers!

Spider venom

Almost all spiders have venom, which they inject into their victims to paralyse them. But very few spiders are actually venomous enough to cause injury to humans. Some of the commonly found venomous spiders that are harmful to humans include black widow, brown recluse and yellow sac spiders. Although the venom of a black widow is considered highly toxic, hardly any death has been reported. The bite can, however, be painful and may cause severe adverse reactions.

Venom kills

Scorpions and centipedes are among the most poisonous creatures on earth. They can kill humans and big animals. Both are often mistaken for bugs, although they do not belong to this family.

INTERESTING FACT!
Killer bees are very dangerous. If their hive is disturbed, they attack anything in the surrounding area. They attack in large numbers and their stings can kill people.

House Creatures

You may not like them a lot, but bugs can feel very much at home in your house! Most of them usually come in uninvited, like flies and mosquitoes. Others like cockroaches have lots of babies and hide in little corners.

Dinner time

Female mosquitoes drink blood, while males only sip plant nectar. Houseflies cannot bite or chew, but they can liquefy many solid foods with their saliva. Cockroaches, on the other hand, are scavengers. They eat food and a variety of other substances, including book binding, paper, soap, plants and dead animals.

■ Certain kinds of mosquitoes carry germs that cause diseases like encephalitis, malaria and yellow fever. When a mosquito bites your body, it may leave germs behind

INTERESTING FACT!

The buzzing of a fly is actually the sound of its wings beating. A housefly's wings beat about 200 times a second. A mosquito makes more sound, with its wings moving about 1,000 times a second.

■ Termites live on trees and have a long, nose-like snout. They can spray glue from their nose, using it to trap other bugs and kill them

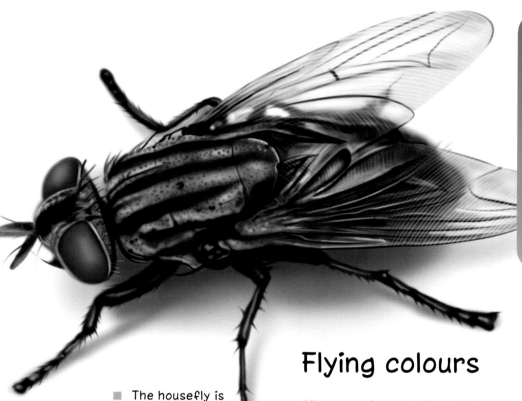

FACT FILE
Housefly
Up to 6-9 mm (0.24-0.35 inches) long; wingspan 13-15 mm (0.51-0.60 inches)
Can fly at 7 kph (4.3 mph)
Mosquito
Average length 3-6 mm (0.12-0.24 inches); can fly at 1.6-2.4 kph (0.99-1.49 mph)
Cockroach
Can run up to 5 kph (3 mph)

■ The housefly is often a carrier of diseases such as typhoid fever, cholera, dysentery and anthrax

Flying colours

Flies can have dull-black, brown, grey, or yellowish bodies, covered with fine hair. A few kinds, including soldier flies and hover flies, may have bright orange, white or yellow markings. Some others, such as bluebottles and green bottles, are shiny blue or green.

Brown and crawly

Cockroaches have flat, oval bodies. Their long legs are covered with bristles that help it to feel. Cockroaches are fast-runners and many of them can fly as well. These bugs have long antennae with organs that can detect certain smells.

Keeping them away

■ A cockroach can hold its breath for 40 minutes. It can also live for a week, even if its head is cut off!

The best way to keep bugs away is to keep the house clean. It is advisable not to keep old newspapers or have stagnating, dirty water collect. Any crack in the wall should be sealed, as young cockroaches can crawl into gaps only 0.5 mm (0.02 inches) wide. One can also use sprays. Mosquitoes and cockroaches are tough survivors, though.

Bugs that Harm

Very few insect species are harmful to humans. Less than one per cent of all bugs are really dangerous. But these few bugs can create a lot of havoc. They eat up our crops, invade our houses and do not spare our clothes and furniture either. They can also infect us with diseases.

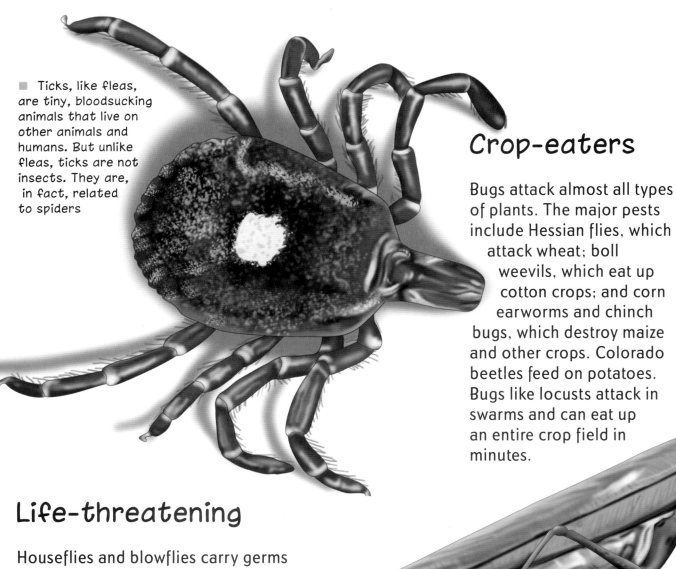

■ Ticks, like fleas, are tiny, bloodsucking animals that live on other animals and humans. But unlike fleas, ticks are not insects. They are, in fact, related to spiders

Crop-eaters

Bugs attack almost all types of plants. The major pests include Hessian flies, which attack wheat; boll weevils, which eat up cotton crops; and corn earworms and chinch bugs, which destroy maize and other crops. Colorado beetles feed on potatoes. Bugs like locusts attack in swarms and can eat up an entire crop field in minutes.

Life-threatening

Houseflies and blowflies carry germs and deposit these in our food or water. They cause diseases like typhoid fever, cholera and dysentery. Insect bites can also cause deadly illnesses like dengue fever, encephalitis, malaria, African sleeping sickness and bubonic plague. Some bugs like fleas and lice live on human bodies and suck our blood.

Home invaders

Bugs create a mess in our homes. Cloth moths and carpet beetles make holes in clothes, sofas and carpets. Silverfish can damage books, while termites eat up anything in wood. Ants and cockroaches spoil our food and can also transport germs.

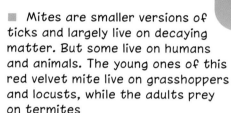

INTERESTING FACT!

Predators, parasites or diseases can be used to check pests. When the cottony cushion bug posed a threat to California's lemon and orange orchards, ladybirds were brought in to eat up the pests.

FACT FILE

A swarm of desert locusts contains over 1,000 million bugs
Swarms can cover an area of about 5,180 square kilometres (2,000 square miles)
Fleas can jump nearly 200 times the length of their bodies
Female mosquitoes can suck blood as much as thrice their body weight

■ Mites are smaller versions of ticks and largely live on decaying matter. But some live on humans and animals. The young ones of this red velvet mite live on grasshoppers and locusts, while the adults prey on termites

Kill them fast!

The easiest way to kill a harmful bug is to swat it the minute you see one! But it is not always safe, especially if bugs are in large numbers. The other option is to use special sprays called insecticides, which kill the pests.

■ Many beetles have been found to be harmful to crops. The rhinoceros beetle is a common pest in the tropical regions. It bores into the trunks and leaves of coconut trees and feeds on the tender tissues

■ The praying mantis is often mistaken for a pest. On the contrary it feeds on other insects, especially crop-eating pests

Bugs that Help

Some bugs can be very helpful for humans. They help in pollination, make products such as honey, feed on harmful bugs, and serve as food for birds and other animals.

Cleaning agents

Bugs help to keep the landscape clean by feeding on animal wastes and dead animals, as also on the remains of dead plants. Bugs that live in the ground enrich the soil with their waste products and dead bodies.

■ Dung beetles eat dung. They either make a ball out of it, or simply dig burrows under or near the food. This eating habit of the dung beetle not only reduces the piles of manure but also improves the quality of soil and helps to control pests and flies

Sweet honey

Honeybees suck up nectar from flowers and store it in their honey stomachs. They return to the hive and spit the nectar back into it. The worker bees in the hive then add enzymes to the nectar. As the water in the nectar evaporates, the nectar changes into honey!

■ Honeybees communicate by dancing. The dance tells worker bees where to find nectar

■ The ladybird eats several kinds of crop-destroying bugs

FACT FILE

Honeybees must tap some 2 million flowers to make 0.5 kg (500 grams) of honey
They fly over 88,514 km (55,000 miles) for 0.5 kg of honey
One average worker honeybee makes just 1/12 teaspoons in her lifetime
Honeybee flies 24 kph (15 mph); visits 50 to 100 flowers in one trip

INTERESTING FACT!

Some helpful bugs act as parasites, living in—or on— the bodies of harmful bugs. For example, some wasps lay their eggs in caterpillars that damage tomato plants. As the young wasps develop, they feed on the caterpillars.

■ If the caterpillar is left to eat its way out of the cocoon naturally, the threads will be cut short and the silk will be useless. So silkworm cocoons are first thrown into boiling water, to kill the silkworms, before opening the cocoons

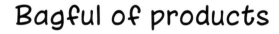

Bagful of products

Bugs provide us with many valuable products. These include honey and beeswax, made by bees; shellac, made from a substance given off by lac bugs; and silk, produced by silkworms.

Spinning silk

A silkworm is not a worm, but the larva of a moth. A silkworm feeds only on mulberry leaves. It spins a cocoon from where raw silk is obtained. The cocoon is made of a single, continuous thread of raw silk, which is 300 metres to 900 metres long.

Glossary

Adaptability: A living organism's ability to change or be changed to suit its surroundings or environment.

Anthrax: An infectious disease found among warm-blooded animals, especially cattle and sheep. It is caused by the bacterium *Bacillus anthracis.*

Aphid: A small, soft-bodied insect of the family Aphididae. It has mouthparts used for piercing and sucking plant sap.

Camouflage: A bug's natural method of concealing itself from an enemy by appearing to be part of its surroundings.

Carrion: A dead or decaying animal.

Cholera: A disease of the small intestine caused by the bacteria *vibrio cholerae.* Symptoms include vomiting, upset stomach, muscle cramps and dehydration.

Dengue: A type of fever found in the tropics. It is caused by mosquitoes and symptoms include rash headaches and joint pain.

Encephalitis: A disease where the patient suffers inflammation of the brain. Symptoms include headache, drowsiness, nausea and fever.

Habitat: An environment where an organism lives and multiplies.

Larva: The wingless, wormlike form of bugs that hatches from eggs.

Lens: A transparent tissue that is found behind the iris in the eye.

Malaria: An infectious disease carried by the Anopheles mosquito. Symptoms include fever and shivering.

Membrane: A sheer tissue that covers or connects organs or cells in living organisms.

Metamorphosis: The total transformation a larva undergoes into its adult stage.

Naiad: A plant that grows underwater; has narrow leaves and small flowers.

Pheromone: A chemical substance that an organism gives out, as a reaction to others of the same species.

Pollination: The process by which pollen is transferred to help a plant reproduce.

Predator: An animal that preys on other animals for its food.

Pupa: The stage of development of an insect between its larva and adult phases.

Species: A group of organisms that have identical traits and can interbreed.

Spinneret: Special organ situated under the abdomen of spiders, used to spin webs.

Yellow fever: Infectious disease caused by a virus carried by the Aedes mosquito. Symptoms include fever, muscle cramps, headache and backache.

Index